THE BASILICA OF TORCELLO AND SANTA FOSCA'S

Texts of the priest Antonio Niero

ARDO/Edizioni d'Arte/Venezia

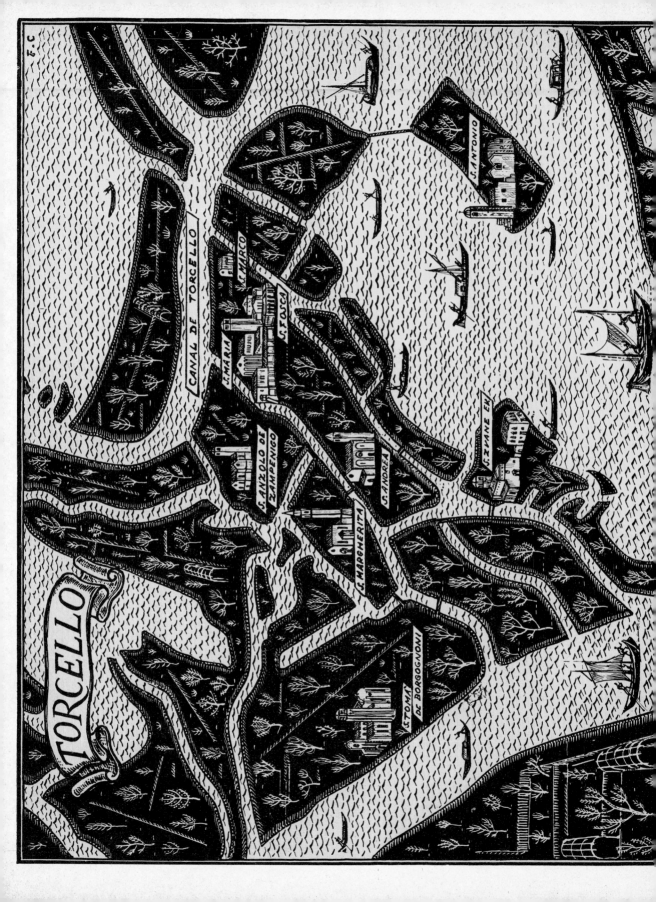

Dear reader,

Many people have written on Torcello and its interesting monuments. Prof. Antonio Niero, well versed in the matter, offers you a historical, artistic guide of S. Maria Assunta's Basilica, a monument famous for its byzantine mosaics and of S. Fosca's church, a characteristic greek-byzantine building.

These wonderful antiques of the ancient town, now formed by a few houses with few inhabitants owing to historical and natural events, are a witness of the grandeur of the glorious, splendid past of Torcello, rich in art and faith.

We present it to you, hoping to please you, but our best thaks are for the author and Marzari Co. which printed it.

May you get the wonderful message these works communicate from these pages.

THE EDITOR

The Basilica and S. Fosca's

By tradition, Torcello (Torcellum) derives its name from one of the ancient gates of the roman town of Altino, which stood in front of the present Torcello, like a small defence tower. As the same name is present in some places of the plain of the Po, it is more probable that also in the lagoon we have to go back to a pre-roman origin, with a meaning of lagoon geography, i.e. a place emerged among the marshes, as the other ancient denomination *Dorceum* can confirm. It was probably inhabited during the roman epoch; at least in the imperial time when some Villas of Altino, remembered by Marziale's famous lines (died in 102), might have been built. In fact owing to the excavations made by the Polish archaeological mission in 1961-62, they ascertained the presence of a roman installation, during the first and second cent. A.C., with traces of houses. During the Vth cent. this installation was destroyed by the adverse geographic conditions; perhaps a strong, rough sea, connected with the disorder of the venetian river regimes submerged everything. In the VIth, VIIth cent. there are new traces of a repopulating, documented by the ruins of a circular furnace, used for the glass manufacture and other activities of bronze and furnishings. But we have got some more important documents. The famous epigraphic inscription, found in the cathedral and kept there, remembers that the Basilica consecrated to Maria, Mother of God was built in 639 for account of Isaac, the exarch of Ravenna; the bishop was perhaps Mauro. It is not worth arguing if this inscription refers to Torcello as scholars affirm, or to Cittanova Eracleiana, near the present Eraclea. It is probable the bishop Mauro led here his faithful running away from Altino, where the Longobards' pressure was intensifying. The same dedication to God's Mother (Theotócos) meant an affirmation of catholic faith against the Arian Longobard likings and the devotedness to the emperor Eraclio, crier of the devotion to God's Mother.

We don't know the plan of this primitive cathedral, Perhaps, it stood on the area of the present one, rebuilt in 1008, with a central apse, included into a perimetric wall, and two rudimentary small apses, according to the upper Adriatic typical lagoon scheme . At the beginning of the XVIIIth cent. the bishop Adeodato I completed the building adorning it with marble decorations, as the chronicler Giovanni Diacono, a well informed source, wrote at the end of the XXth cent. Other important works were made by the bishop Adeodato II (864-867); the prolongation of the central apse beyond the perimetric wall, the enlargement of the two small side apses, of the crypt and the porch before the facade. About 1000 the bishop Orso Orseolo, the son of the Doge Pietro Orseolo II, a true follower of his family's tradition, who had taken an interest in holy buildings (his grandfather, the Doge Orseolo I, the Saint, had rebuilt S. Marco's), gave the basilica the present shape, by heightening the central nave, opening some windows in the west wall and the facade and by heightening the floor and building new columns and the ciborium on the altar, later demolished. He erected the majestic bell tower, too. So we remember three buildings of Torcello cathedral: the first in 639 (of which it remains only the low part of the facade, completed at the end of the cent.); the second in 864-867, due to the bishop Adeodato II of which it remains some present elements; the third, wanted by the bishop Orso Orseolo, about 1008, still showing itself in the superb architectonic greatness. During the following centuries many other elements adorned it; by the end of 1100 and the beginning of 1200 they probably built the present mosaics, the central apse, the back facade, and the right apse and by the end of 1200 the silver altar-piece, now gone to ruin and placed in the near museum and in the XIII cent. the plutei of the three door wall (iconostasi) coming from S. Marco's Basilica, according to a recent hypothesis. In 1423, under the bishop Pietro Nani, there was a general restoration of the basilica and the present pictures of the partition wall were probably painted by Zanino di Pietro in this occasion. There were other restorations in 1646, when a thunderbolt damaged the cathedral, the bell tower and the episcopate, seriously, and other works of consolidation in 1821 and 1827 according to the emperor of Austria, Francesco Primo's will and finally from 1929-39 the two buildings, the Cathedral and S. Fosca, were brought again to their primary lines, ridding them of baroque superstructures. In fact, after the Council of Trente they inserted the typical devotions of that time, such as the altar of S. Liberale, of Assunta, with an altar-piece of Tintoretto, on the left; the Innocents' altar with an altar-piece of Veronese and S. Teonisto's, on the right; the high altar, erected in 1629 according to the projects of Baldassare Longhena and demolished in 1929 to build the present one. The ciborium was destroyed in 1629; the silver altar-piece was put on the partition wall and S. Eliodoro's urn was put over the altar, supported by angelic children's figures (perhaps by Moli) with two angels on the sides, of the school of Longhena and a statue of the Saint, which was replaced by S. Lorenzo Giustiniani's during the XVIIIth cent. The two altars of the side small apses were added in the XIXth cent. Torcello lost its importance as episcopal see and title in 1818 for it was joined to the patriarchate of Venice, it depends upon now, and keeps only the dean title consecrated to S. Maria Assunta (perhaps after 1100); its inhabitants are only one hundred, the glorious rest of one of the most ancient lagoon markets before 1000, celebrated by Costantino Porfirogenito, emperor of Bisanzio, but declined when its activities were gradually absorbed by the rising Venice.

▶
1 - The Isle of Torcello in its lagoon

The Basilica

THE BAPTISTERY

In front of the cathedral there are the remains of the baptistery. It was probably a circular plan building, with an octogonal colonnade inside, forming an annular corridor; in the middle, under a vault, there was the basin for the baptism dipping, administered according to the ancient liturgy at Easter night and whit Sunday one.

We can still see two big niches near the central door, which perhaps contained two altars, the marble threshold, the bases of the columns and traces of painted plaster and the side door. Its plan has no comparison with similar buildings in the Adriatic, but we must go back to Salona of to Siria. Anyhow the plan is typically roman with byzantine annotations, noticeable in the two large side niches, that you can see also in S. Donato of Zara and after 1000, in the roman Cathedral at Iesolo. It is placed before the central door with an evident liturgical introduction function of the catechumens and new christians to the Cathedral. It goes back to the VIIth cent.

THE BASILICA

The present building, i.e. the Orseolo's of 1008, 50 m. long and 21 m. large has three aisles with a heightened central facade, three doors and a front portico of the IXth cent. leaning against the baptistery. It is supported by six round and square columns and opens partly in a full sail vault and partly lean-to roof. In earlier times the colonnade included only four columns; two on the right and two on the left of the baptistery, in the XIVth cent. the woody trusses were modified in the buttress present one, and during the XVth cent. they added two columns on the right side, which joined the porch with the one of the near martyrium of S. Fosca, forming a unitary whole; later, on the left side they added a prolongation in relation to the entrance to the Schola Episcopalis (a room of the brotherhood, with some remains of frescoes). Among the three doors, the jamb of the main entrance decorated with reliefs, deserve a particular attention; on the right there are bunches of grapes, rosettes, and a candelabrum floral interlacing of the period of Orseolo; adove a vine-shoot with grapes and vine-leaves of a previous period, perhaps of the IXth cent. and on the left, geometrical volutes with crosslets, of the period of Orseolo. On the wall there are two remains of a pluteus, perhaps of the IXth cent., and the last door on the left lets in the storehouses added in the XVIth cent. On the right there is a neoclassic Crucifixion of little value; a memorial tablet in honour of Francesco Primo, emperor of Austria, who, thanks to

2 - *Sight from the plane of the Basilica of Torcello and S. Fosca*

Pyrker (1821-1827), the Patriarch of Venice began the restoration of S. Fosca's Cathedral and the bell tower.

Above the portico there is the brick principal facade, divided into six pillars cut horizontally a little above the connection of the two small side aisles perhaps where the prospect of the IXth cent. ended, creating the illusion of a gallery; it is a whole of Ravenna taste where the wall has a decorative function, getting, in conseguence a sense of brightness due to the grazing shaking of light, which forms some shade plays, according to Bettini's subtle interpretation. Correspondently with the fourth and the fifth pillar there are, above, two bull's eye small windows, built by the Orseolo in 1008 for practical purposes. These ones and the two windows supported by centrings of the second and fifth pillar, opened already in the IXth cent, were closed later, because of the mosaic of the inside wall. You can see the same windows supported by centrings in the two fronts of the small side aisles, built along all the space of the pillars and later blinded. It is possible to remark the persistence of the symbolic motive based on the value of three, the holy number, with reference to the Trinity. Adove, near the typanum there is Pietro Nani, the local bishop's coat of arms, in memory of the restorations of the Cathedral in 1423.

THE INSIDE

You enter the Cathedral through a side door (the remains of two rosette and plait plutei perhaps of the IXth cent. are driven in the wall, while the two inscriptions remembering the church consecration feast are of the XVIth cent.) and feel pervaded by the solemnity of the whole. The light falling through the ten side windows of the central nave, open only on the south part both for a greater lighting and in defence of North cold winds, wherefore the North side has a continued wall, determine, in the colour decomposition of the wall bricks and the reflections of the floor mosaic, an effect of space division of lagoon taste. If there were not the chains amid the columns, a byzantine reminiscence, due already in the period of Orseolo, to technical necessities, to withstand the wall disbanding caused by the ground, according to a rule, frequent in the roman-gothic Venetian churches, the whole would certainly recall S. Apollinare Nuovo in Ravenna. They perhaps wanted to cover the walls of the central nave with mosaics to join the apse and the entrance, but they probably lacked money. The central nave is separated from the side aisles by nine greek marble columns, on each side, with veinings caused by weather and climate; between the seventh and the ninth there is the presbytery, according to a paleochristian, upper Adriatic proceeding that may be found in S. Tommaso di Pola's, too. Almost all the columns are the bishop Orseolo's work, who in part used pre-existing elements; the corinthian capitals are composed in double turn of soft acanthus supporting a low capital and the arches, bordered red according to a lagoon taste. The second and the sixth right capitals are vine-twig and ovule crown ones (VIth cent.), used in the rebuilding of 1008; while the five capitals near the apse are of the Xth cent; The large, present floor, Orseolo's work, is 30 cm. higher than the one of the IXth cent., worked in white-black small cubes and divided into squares as we can see from the excavations of 1939; on the contrary, the present one develops, in the presbitery, in a pretious, geometric play realized in the XIIIth cent. perhaps coeval of the entrance wall mosaics. On the walls of the right small aisle there are two altars; the first of the second part of the XVIth cent. with « The Massacre of the Innocents » a painting of the school of Veronese; the second in a fine polychrome wood intaglio of Paolo Campsa (at the beginning of the XVIIth cent.) modified by Antonio de Poris, shows the bishop Teonisto, the ancient patron of Altino, in the middle; on its sides there are S.

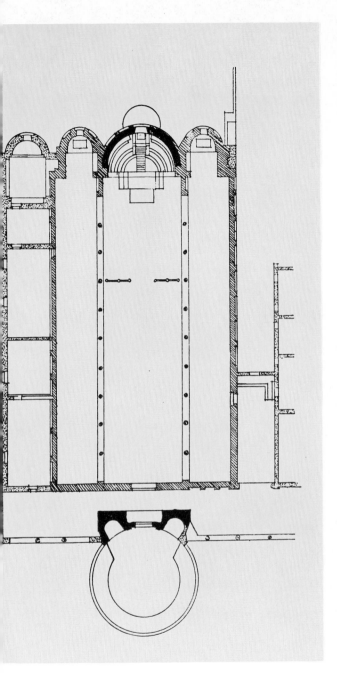

THE PLAN OF THE CATHEDRAL WITH THREE
AISLES AND THE APSE IN FRONT OF THE BAPTI-
STERY.
The walls marked in black colour belong to the first con-
struction of the VII century. The remainders to the fol-
lowing rebuildings.

THE CENTRAL APSE OF THE CATHEDRAL IN
VERTICAL SECTION, WITH THE CRYPTE BELOW,
OBTAINED UNDER THE PRESBYTERIAL EXEDRA.

3 - *The inside of the Cathedral seen from the central nave after the remaking in 1008, under the Bishop Orso Orseolo*

▶
4/5 - *Two details of the floor of the Cathedral of the XIth cent.*

3

Antonio and S. Nicola di Bari; above, the Annunciation in reliefs; in the middle there are scenes of the Saint's martyrdom (his preaching and beheading) below, there are the Adoration of the Magi and the Circumcision. Near the entrance small door there is the Madonna with the Child, of a roman master of the XIIIth cent. Near the presbitery there are the bishop Paolo di Altino's tombstone and the partition wall with the holy door in the middle of it, obtained by three small columns half closed by the precious marble plutei and supporting the scenes of the twelve Apostles with the Virgin, attributed by Roberto Longhi to Zanino di Pietro (1423) who worked in Venice at the beginnings of the XVth cent. On the plutei there are two young lions near a tree, marshy ducks pecking the green and two hares playing on the ground; six convolvulus are on the upper part. Two peacocks are catching some grapes, in a vase supported by a tall column, on a ground of curled up and closed leaf vine-tendrils. Some scholars have lately put forth the hypothesis these plutei belonged to the building of the present S. Marco's, moved here, to Torcello, when during the XIIIth cent. they rebuilt the partition wall in S. Marco, in the present shape. The executive preciosity of the whole, obtained by using the drill, with an evident reference to the ivory techniques, and to the same Bisanzio, from where they suppose the creator had arrived, is very noticeable.

The twelve Apostles of the partition wall are: on the right S. Paolo, S. Bartolomeo, S. Giacomo Maggiore, illegible, S. Filippo, S. Giacomo Minore, on the left, S. Pietro, S. Andrea, illegible, and S. Simone, illegible. On the left there is the pulpit, of the XI and XIIth cent. near the presbytery and the aisle of the congregation. Like the ones of Grado and S. Marco, it stands on the right of the altar.

According to Lorenzetti the present arrangement of the pulpit is not the original one, but a following change. At the time of Orseolo there were two pulpits; one on the right side of the choir to read the epistle and one on the left side for the Gospel with double ladder to reach them.

Perhaps, when in 1200 they modified the plutei, employing the present ones, the two pulpits were blended in the present shape, cutting and sawing the decorative marble plates. The first, supported by a polygonal small column used for the epistle the second, with a richer decoration for the Gospel, rests on four columns according to the west scheme; the platform is formed of polychrome marbles and column parapets to let the congregation see the choir and the clergy; around the choir-stand, standing on a small column, there are some human small heads acting as a decorative and a support. The marble plate, protecting the entrance steps on the side of the aisle, has a central floral motive framed by a dentil and tress bundle of the same style and work of the plutei. The huge woody crucifix of the XVth cent. with a rung cross rises on the perpendicular chain of the partition wall.

When you enter the presbytery you see the woody, felze inlaid choir stalls of the clergy, of the XVth cent., the mosaic floor and the right venetian-byzantine plutei (XIth cent.) with a vine rich in leaves and bunches pecked by four gulls; the first on the left represents the pagan myth of Issione, sentenced to death in the XIth cent. the present altar was rebuilt because of the restorations in 1939 on a primitive scheme with different materials found during the works; the altar slab is formed of thick greek marble. Once, in its place, there was a huge baroque building, erected in 1629. In front of it, defended by a lattice, there is the grave of the martyr or *fenestrella confessionis*, protecting a roman sarcophagus of the IInd-IIIrd cent. B.C., brought from Altino by the refuges in 639, keeping the remains of S. Eliodoro, the bishop of Altino, S. Girolamo's friend.

6 - *Detail of the partition wall - XV th cent.*

7 - *The « Pluteus of the Peacoks » - A Venetian-Byzantine relief which represents two peacocks drinking at the source of Eternal Life - XIth cent.*

8 - *The « Pluteus of the Lions ». A Venetian-Bizantine relief of the XIth cent. which forms, as the previous one, a parapet in the partition wall of the Cathedral*

7   8

9 - *A woody Crucifix of the XIth cent.*

10 - *The Pulpit of the Cathedral, near the partition wall, placed here and renewed in the XII-XIIIth cent.*

▶
11 - *The mosaic of the central Apse. In the middle of the golden conch there is the Virgin with the Blessing Child; below there are twelve Apostles, over the triumphal arch the Annunciation - XIIth-XIIIth cent.*

Behind the altar there is the apse basin characterized by several elements; first of all the bishop's throne, rising above six circular flights of stairs. Ten steps, with a clear call to the Ten Commandments lead to it. The system of leaning the episcopal throne against the bottom apse is still of the Upper Adriatic, as it is present in S. Maria delle Grazie in Grado of the Vth cent. as working out of a west or Syriac system and in S. Irene's church in Costantinopoli. The clergy placed themselves on the side steps, in the course of solemn rites or councils, according to the liturgic order; deacons, subdeacons acolyte exorcists, door-keepers, lectors. From the throne the cathedral appears much wider and longer; from there the bishop had the impression of being really the helmsman of his people and island. On the right side there are some inscriptions, one in honour of the bishop Marco Zeno in remembrance of the removal of the holy bodies; on the left there is an inscription of 629, a precious document on the history of Torcello and the lagoons.

Above the steps and the throne there was a series of frescoes, come to light during the restorations of 1939, of benedectine style, near the ones of the crypt of Aquileia, dealing with the subject of the Saints near Christ. Perhaps they were covered with a series of big plates in the XIIth cent. In the middle, perpendiculary on the episcopal throne there is the modern remaking mosaic of S. Eliodoro, the ancient patron of Torcello diocese, he who joins the militant church with the triumphant one, according the medieval canonic conception. In fact above him it goes on a paradisiac procession of the Apostles, ending in the hieratic, beautiful figure of God's mother. These mosaics were remade, for the most part, at the end of last cent; but they still keep an undoubted value. The Apostles proceed, in alternate symmetry in the low folds of the priestly planet, on a meadow where the five or six flower red weeds, a typical plant of the lagoon prairies, bloom.

They are dressed like the Apostles of Ravenna, each of them with his own symbol, divided six by six with S. Paolo, Matteo, Andrea, Giacomo, Mattia, Filippo, on the right and S. Pietro, Giovanni, Giacomo maggiore, Bartolomeo, Taddeo; Tommaso on the left.

The centre is occupied by the east small window, symbol of Crist *oriens ex alto* and the Virgin, east door in the prophet Ezechiele's opinion, in fact the explanation *porta salutis* coincides with the side of the window. Above, it runs, within a fascia, the invocation in Leonine verse inspired to S. Bernardo from Chiaravalle's doctrine of the Blessed Virgin: *Formula virtutis, maris astrum, porta salutis, prole Maria levat, quas coniunge subdidit Eva.* (Mary, Formula of virtue, Sea star, Salvation door, sets free, with her Son, those whom Eva and Adam reduced to sin.) The sublime figure of God's Mother, Móter Then, as the abbreviation in greek says, prevails in the apse basin within concentric zones of gilt mosaic narrowing slowly on high. According to the byzantine scheme of the Odegetria, she comes down gliding gently from the sky in the revelation of the Divinity. It rests on the worship footstool, decorated with twelve gems, while the right knee scarcely reveals the descent movement.

She is dressed like a queen, with the « Maphorion » on her head, the small cross on her forehead, repeating on the shoulders, and the ample blue peplum with gilt fringes. A rigid neck supports a thin face with scarcely pronounced lips, very mild but motionless eyes, fixed on the bystanders that, the more you look at them, the more they get life and force, making us forget the reality, space and time in which we live, in a rapid foretasting of the Eternal. Also the Child, holding the roll of the law on his gown, is very pleasant. He is dressed like « basileus » and rests on the Virgin's right arm, from whose hand a white handkerchief, *Mater Dolorosa's*

▶ *12 - A detail of the central Apse. The Virgin with the blessing Child (XII-XIIIth cent.)*

ᴹᴿ̄ ΘV̄

PORTA SALVTIS PROLE MARIE SCS

symbol hangs: in this way all the elements of the Redemption gather in Mary. On the frame of the arch it still runs the invocation in latin leonine verse *sum Deus atque caro, patris et sum matris imago, non piger ad lapsum set flentis proximus adsum* (I am God and man, the image of Father and Mother, I am not far from the offender, but I am near the penitent).

The mosaic of the Virgin on the apse is perhaps of 1230, the Apostles' mosaics are of 1100, with evident reference to the mosaic techniques of the Church of Aghias Loukas in the greek Phocis. The Annunciation is told on the royal arch plumes, opening the apse. The Angel Gabriele, on the left, is seen in rapid motion, with his arms stretched; on the right the Virgin, long and thin, is caught in the agitation movement and turns pale at the salutation. With her left hand raised and the right one holding the spindle, she stands up from the throne, wrapped in an ample peplum; she lays the shell-drawn work-basket according to the Annunciation usual scheme in Byzantine area, on the ground.

Also this mosaic reveals the same techniques, and perhaps the same hand of the apse, therefore it is of the same period. On the left wall there is an inscription of the first church building, in 639, a precious and rare lagoon epigraphic document; on the right there are some inscriptions of members of the local clergy. Along the corridor leading to the apse of the right side chapel or diaconicon, on the wall, there is a neoclassic small tabernacle for the relics of the Cross and S. Cecilia's head with a shovel of the Cross symbols; the rest is a work of 1500, as the date below proves. The apse of the chapel is full of mosaics. The mosaic is one of the most passionate problems of historical criticism both for the date and the style. Below, it shows the four doctors of the Latin Church blessing i.e. from the right S. Agostino, S. Ambrogio, S. Martino, S. Gregorio Magno, with a small window opened to the East, symbol of the Christ, in the middle.

It is interesting to notice that S. Martino has taken the place of S. Gerolamo perhaps because of the fame and devotion of the French saint in the Middle Ages and the Torcello lagoon after 1000. The first two saints on the right wear brilliant episcopal clothes with ample planets and palliums, while, the two on the left are dressed in pontificals with a crossed golden decoration, a closed book and a maniple in S. Gregorio. They are separated by the tuft of corn poppies in blossom interlaced in different ways.

On high, there is the latin inscription, inspired to some literary texts of the pagan writer Marziano Cappella and to S. Paolino d'Aquileia: Personis triplex Deux est: et Numine simplex, herbidat hic terram, mare fundit, luminat aetheram (God is triple as to persons but one in the Essence. He covers ground with grass, distributes the seas and illuminates the sky).

The mosaic has a didactic function and completes the one of the high apse, where the Apostles represent the Revelation through the Scriptures and the Doctors of the Church through the Tradition, here. They are a very beautiful work, remade at the end of the XIIth cent. on a probable scheme of the IXth cent. The Christ on the throne masters above, in the apse basin, as a lesgilator surrounded by two angels, Michele on the left and Gabriele on the right, like the ones in S. Giusto's in Trieste. The blessing Christ is sitting on an inlaid throne and rests his bare feet on the cloud-worked footstool with the thunderbolt signs. The bearded, stern face follows the byzantine schemes of 1000; it presents the christian version of the pagan theme, i.e. of the Thunderer, the king of Olympus, while here he is the king of the sky and the earth. The whole is of the XIIth and XIIIth cent. but of a different hand from the inferior mosaic.

13 - *A detail of the central Apse. The six Apostles of the right side (XII-XIIIth cent.)*

14 - *A detail of the central Apse. The six Apostles of the left side (XII-XIIIth cent.)*
▶
15 - *In the following page a sight of the right aisle.*

After admiring the geometric embroidery decoration of the apse border look at the important mosaic of the vault. In the four sails of the crossing, four angels support the shield with the mystic lamb. The ones on the left and the right with serene faces stand on a globe (a ball or a world) on the capital of a column; the ones on high and down, with nervous, hieratic faces, are truncated at their calves perhaps owing to the vault rearrangement works made during Orseolo's period.

The nimbus-girded lamb, in the blue night sky, with his right hand holds the base of the pastoral cross, hooked under the cross-piece, piercing through his breast, from where the redeeming Blood spouts, while he turns on one side with a vigorous dash. Four flowery bands (symbol of the four rivers of the earthly Paradise) fall from the vegetable plait surrounding him, with lilies, bunches of grapes, wheat grains, alluding to the eucharistic mystery, for which the chapel or diaconicon was used. Within the sails there is a luxuriant floral decoration with ample volutes among which sea-gulls and marshy birds fly and a lynx moves with soft pace; below, on the right and left there are sea-gulls, an eagle, a lion, a bull and a peacock that, if as symbol they allude to the Evangelists, as type they correspond to the identical decoration in the presbyteral vault of S. Vitale's in Ravenna, of the IVth cent. The iconographic motive and the stylistic technique of this mosaic and the one of Ravenna are alike, so the mosaic of Torcello was supposed to be a little later, i.e. contemporary of the first building of the Churches, a work of the workmen of Ravenna. Thus it is perhaps the most ancient mosaic of Venetian lagoons, even if it was restored many a time in the XIIth cent. On the left side of the chapel there is a small tabernacle for the holy oils, with shells and two beautiful dolphins, a part of the primitive building of the VIIth cent. much alike the one in the Eufrasiana of Parenzo. The altar is a fine example of baroque with marble inlaid work; the silver small door is a work of the living Remigio Barbaro from Burano. Then through the small wall door you pass into the annular vault of the central apse, communicating with the left one; now it is impossible to pass because of the stagnant water. There is nothing important in the left apse of the presbytery, except the altar of the XVIIth cent. with the tender stone statues of the Saints: Lorenzo Giustiniani, already on the high altar and S. Antonio from Padua (right) and a pictures of S. Antonio from Padua. On the right of the left aisle there are some graves of canons and in the arch niche, remains of a fresco of the XIIth cent. and of an inscription in honour of the bishop Bono Baldo, died in 1215.

The entrance to the pulpits opens on the left with the typical stairs and the decorative plates of the base. It deserves a particular attention the broken fragment, dealing with the pagan subject of the occasion or *cairos*, running away, while the old, lazy man, smoothing his beard, tries to keep it and a lazy woman grieves for the lost occasion; on the contrary, the bold young man seizes the time and stops it without any indecision. It is of the XIth cent. with roman anticipations and was already a part of the decoration of the most ancient pulpit. Near the door of the sacristy there is a small holy- water basin of the IXth cent.; tre woody altar of Campsa, like the right one, with S. Liberale in the middle, S. Girolamo on the left and S. Antonio from Padua on the right and, below, scenes of the life of S. Liberale and the altar with the shovel of the Virgin, a work of Jacopo Tintoretto. The large mosaic of the wall is worked according to byzantine rules, so that the congregation going out of the church bears the memory of the last destiny according to the warning of the Scriptures: « *remember your last destiny and you will sin no longer.* » (Eccl. 7, 40).

▶
16 - The Right side chapel of the Holy Sacrament. Below there are the four doctors of the Church: S. Gregorio and Martino - S. Agostino and S. Ambrogio; in the central part there are the blessing Saviour on the throne and the Archangels Michele and Gabriele; above: four angels support the Copper Shield with the Mystic Lamb - XIIth cent.

17 - The Holy Sacrament's Apse: S. Martino blessing; one of the four doctors of the Church.

18 - The Holy Sacrament's Apse: S. Ambrogio. A mosaic, on a golden background, for the most part rebuilt on a more ancient plan, in the XIIth cent.

▶

19 - Another detail of the mosaic of the Holy Sacrament's Chapel: the blessing Saviour on the throne.

It is divided into two large parts both for subject reasons and for style ones: the inferior one represents scenes of the last judgment in the first, second, third, fourth fascia and was performed in the second part of the XIIth cent.; the upper one deals with the mystery of Christ's death and his descent to the hell in the fifth and sixth fascia and was performed later, at the beginning of the XIIth cent. For an easier reading follow the proposed division. In the fourth fascia within the almond there is the Christ judge with the Passion wounds; the chest is not bare yet, for this scheme, a German contribution, appears in the following cent; on the sides there are the Virgin and Battista protected by two angels of the Domiration choir, wearing a richly studded with gems clothes.

Two angels of the throne choir support the divine almond and above, the four tetraform beings, remember the four Evangels, according to the scheme of the Syriac miniatures of Rabula. The biblical river of fire, already described by the Syriac poet Commodiano di Gazza, of the IV cent. springs from the almond gurgling and curling in the space to feed the hell below. The twelve Apostles are sitting on a long sofa on the side of Christ, like in the picture of the Vatican picture-gallery, at fixed seats, decorated with fusaroles; they are six on each side, led, on the right, by S. Pietro with the keys and on the left by S. Paolo, holding the book of the epistles.

In the middle of the third fascia it dominates the « Etimasia » or triumph of the cross, placed over the clouds, according to S. Matteo's apocalyptic text, with the symbols of the passion: the lance, the sponge, the crown of thorns and the book of Life put on the altar. Two seraphs keep the cross and two Principati (Angels) the Etimasia, while below the frightened Adam and Eva, symbol of all the tribes of the earth in terror and tears, according to S. Matteo's narration, are worshipping.

On the left and right four angels with blaring trumpets of the kind of the one of the Carolingian Horn, call the death to the resurrection: these, wrapped in their sindons, on the left, come out of the sepulchres and the throats of wild beasts (lions, elephant, hyena, griffons and ravens) like in the Vatican picture.

On the right, the dead of the sea, victims of wrecks rise, in a clear language for a people of sailors and fishermen such as the inhabitants of Torcello.

The womanly figure, emerging from the sea monster with links on her arms and legs, is the symbol of the sea, according to the byzantine scheme. The angel unrolling a roll, is dissipating the starry sky which will fall at the end of times, according to S. Matteo's texts. In the middle of the second fascia S. Michele is weighing the Souls in the classic aspect of the « psicostasia », a theme dear to the East figuration, with the horned demons, trying to make the scale lean to them, throwing the sins from their leather bags; a particular, frequent in the west art from Burgundy to Ireland and Sweden. On the right and the left God rewards or punishes. The legions of the Blessed, in four groups, celebrate Christ for the prize. In the first group on the right there are 14 clergymen among which we can identify: S. Gregorio di Nazianzo and S. Basilio with black beard and hair; in the second group there are 13 martyrs preceded by the richly clothed Saint Teodoro followed by S. Giorgio, S. Demetrio, S. Procopio and perhaps S. Teodoro soldier; in the third group there are eleven monks in Basil clothes, where it is possible to recognize S. Autimio with a bifid very long beard and perhaps S. Antonio priest and S. Saba; in the fourth group there are 14 women, the first is a penitent with long, thin legs and arms (perhaps S. Maria Egiziaca), the second is a nun and the third is perhaps S. Caterina from Alessandria with gems on her head, dressed like the Giovannina of S. Teodoro's train in S. Vitale in Ravenna.

▶
20 - The Apse of the Holy Sacrament's Chapel: four angels support the Copper Shield with the Mystic Lamb. This mosaic, conceived on a Roman-Ravenna composite scheme was renewed in the XII cent.

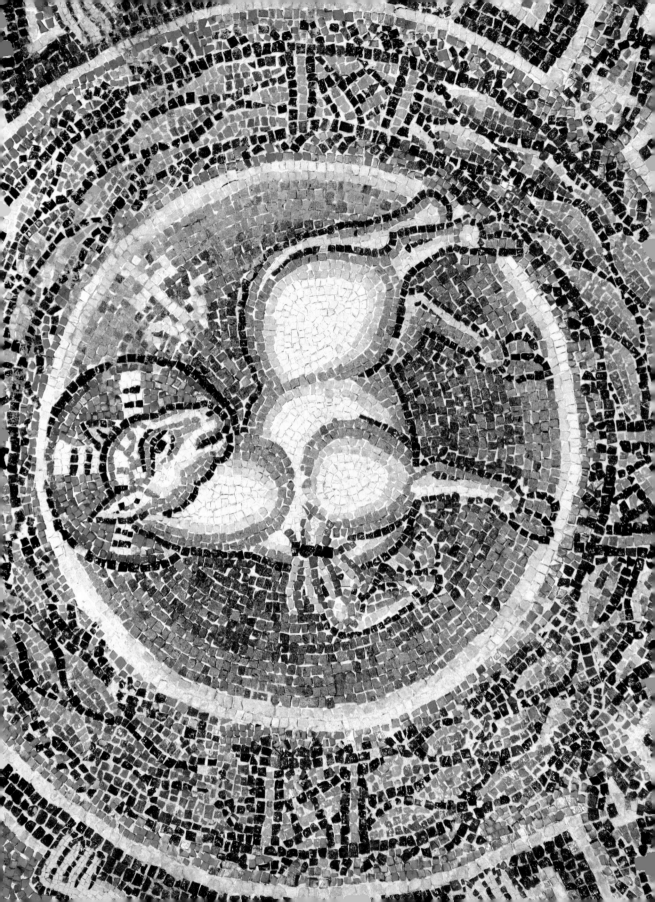

21 - *The Apse of the Holy Sacrament's Chapel: four angels support the Copper Shield with the Mystic Lamb. This mosaic, conceived on a Roman-Ravenna composite scheme was renewed in the XII cent.*

▶
22 - *A decorative detail of the mosaic of the right side Chapel.*

23 - *A detail of the mosaic of the Doomsday: crucified Christ between the Virgin and S. John Evangelist.*

▶

24 - *The large mosaic of the Doomsday in six zones; it occupies the whole bottom facade of the Cathedral. It is a mosaic of Venetian-Byzantine school built in two times, in the XII and XIIIth cent.*

25 - *A detail of the « Doomsday ». The « Deisis »
Christ Judge between the Virgin and S. Giovanni
Battista, in the glory of the heavenly court.*

▶
26/27 - *Details of the « Doomsday »; the group of
the Apostles near the Christ Judge, behind the angelic groups.*

28 - Detail of
« Doomsday ». « L...
toimasia ». The D...
ne throne prepa...
for the Orde...
worhipped by Ad...
and Eva and prot...
ted by the two ...
changels Michele a...
Gabriele.

◀▶

29/30 - Detail ...
the « Doomsday ...
The Resurrection ...
the Dead. On ...
left the call to life ...
the dead from ...
abysses of the s...
on the right the d...
resuscitated from ...
land.

On the left, two red angels, with impassible faces drive the damned into the fire of the hell by long perches. They are the offenders of pride, punished by seven little devils, allusive to the seven main sins of which pride is the source.

According to a probable interpretation the heresiarchs and politicians are punished here. The emperor, pushed by the angel, is perhaps Costantino I Capronimo (741-775), iconoclast identical in a coeval coin; the bald bishop with a fluent beard is the heretic Nestorio, as he appears in the final judgment at Salamina. On high there is a monk with the beard drawn to the right by a little devil with a despiteful relish, who is perhaps the heretic Eutiche; it follows a head with a slightly grey beard, a casque with mark of gems on top and a headgear, or skiadion hanging by his side; he is perhaps the patriarch of Constantinople Sergio (610-638) an heretic supporter of monothelism, the little devil tries to uncrown. Then there are a diademed queen or basilissa, perhaps the empress Eudossia, who persecuted Crisostomo and that an impertinent devil tries to uncrown and a nun, whose wimple is seized by a devil, gesticulating towards Lucifer. A young man with a west headgear, a prominent chin in the act of making faces, turns to Lucifer.

On his right, another devil seizes an old, bearded man with a coloured or fringed band arab headgear and below a little devil with his hand stretched towards Lucifer in symmetry with the left one, is dragging a men. Lucifer or Ades is sitting in the middle, according to the byzantine scheme. His throne is the back of the biblical monster or Leviathan with very bright blue scales and two heads of he-goat, the devils' symbol as, a century later, the liturgy sings in Dies Irae; it is devouring two women. In his lap on a green flap, symbol of the hope in evil, he carries the Antichrist, as a byzantine basileus, a blasphemous opposition to the Virgin Odegetria of the central apse; Lucifer has his right hand stretched and the Antichrist's replies to his gesture.

Below the throne there are two heads: a man with moustaches, a deformed ear with pendants, plait hair falling from the bare occiput, therefore Mongol and opposite an Egyptian woman, with a polychrome arab turban, and a high blue collar. As we see, it is evident here the principle of deeming damned those who are not baptized, especially the supporters of Islam, echo of the byzantine struggles against them, but in symbolic function of the pagans, at Torcello. Below, in the first fascia the damned suffer, according to the medieval law of retaliation: the lustful among the blazes; an old man, perhaps the rich Epulone, a young man and an old man with a bifid beard (perhaps a Northman); four naked gluttons biting their hands; two wrathful, an old man smoothing his beard and a young haloed man dipped in deep, cold waters; the envious people, reduced to 17 skulls with the imps penetrating into the empty eye- sockets; the misers presented with eleven cut heads; four of them are women's with ear-rings; the decoration of four men's heads with different parting hair and the typical moustaches, still recalls the Mongolian race; then, there are the indolent, ten, considering bones, hands and cut feet. The sense of horrid and macabre predominates in the two scenes of envious and indolent people; it finds a correspondence in the byzantine frescoes of the final judgment in the Apostles' church at Amari, in Creta, a little later than the work of Torcello, as well in the episode of the resurrection of the dead in the Vatican painting already mentioned. As you can see there are the seven main vices in the punishments of Hell, according to the scheme of west theology in relation with the seven little devils already seen; the three main concupiscences, rememberd by S. Giovanni are painted red in the squares: the concupiscence of the flesh (the lustful), the concupiscence of the eyes (the misers), the pride of

▶
31 - Detail of the « Doomsday ». The Angel holding the scales, where men's good and bad actions will be weighed

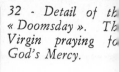

32 - Detail of th
« Doomsday ». Th
Virgin praying to
God's Mercy.

33 - Detail of th
« Doomsday ». Th
Bishops, the Martyrs
the Monks the hol
women, predestina
ted to the heavenl
Beatitude, pray to
God's mercifulness.

34 - Detail of the « Doomsday » - The Hell: Lucifer, the Great Proud, seated on a dragon, keeps his son, the Antichrist, on his knees, while the two Angels drive the proud into the fire by their lances.

35 - Detail of the « Doomsday » - The Damned of the Hell; the Lustful: The Gluttons - the Choleric - the Envious People - the Misers - the Indolent

life (the proud). Opposite there is the paradise, the soil of which is covered with corn poppies. S. Peter keeps the keys and S. Michele is represented as « psicopompo » i.e. leader of souls; near the Paradise door there is a cherub, whose wings are quilted with eyes, while the Good Robber, on the other side, holds the salvation cross.

Then it appears a woman praying, it is perhaps the Virgin. It follows the groups of the elected, portrayed in twelve, according to the text of the Apocalypse (Apoc. 7) among the 12,000 shown to indicate the saved, sent to the Old Man, carrying the Saviour in his lap, opposite as to technique and figure to the Antichrist of the Hell, and then Abraham and his bosom, according to the byzantine schema and the west liturgy motive of the dead. In the lunette, in the middle, there is the Virgin praying or Mother of Mercy with the invocation: *Virgo, divinum natum prece pulsa, terge reatum* (Virgin, pray the divine Child; cleanse from the sins).

Her look is firm and penetrating like the « pendant » of the Mother of God in the apse basin. The second part of the mosaic, i.e. the upper one shows no specific characters on the Crucifixion as it was completely remade by the end of last cent., but the scene of the Descent to the Hell and the Resurrection has a great interest both for iconography and date. The scheme is always byzantine according to the monk Dionigi from Furna's rules at section 306 of this « Treatise on painting » but with some west iconographic annotations. Christ, holding the triumphal cross, has broken the doors of the Hell and tramples upon the devil crouching like a larva under him, very different from the stout one of the mosaic of Daphni in Greece in the XIth cent., while locks and keys are scattered everywhere.

He is holding out his hand to the old Adam, Eva is praying with a coquetry-plaited veil on her head, and a mild face different from the bitter one in Delphi.

On the right Battista, wearing an ample gown points at the resuscitated Christ. Behind him there are the 16 prophets, i.e. the four main (perhaps the first white-bearded is Isaia) and the twelve minor; on the left there are the two haloed kings, David and Salomon, after the Greek rite. Beneath the two groups in two hollows of mount; two young groups, three by three, wearing white tunics, rise their hands to Christ; this particular wants in the scene of Daphni as well in the one to Nea Moni of Chios and is perhaps of west origin, certainly from the Gospel of Nicodemo, but mediated by the apocryphal sermon 160 of Pascha, of S. Agostino and by the west liturgy of the dead, where they insist on the « plausus » of the dead. Also the presence of greek explanations (*E Anastasis*) the only ones in the whole wall, but near the identical proceedings in S. Mark's mosaics, and some stylistic particulars such as the timid presence of the arrow style in Eva's plaits, in Adam, and Christ, his nimbus with gems and his oval face, lead us to date the mosaic in the first part of the XIIth cent. coeval of the apse Virgin. The large mosaic cycle, of venetian technique, even if of remote Syriac origins, presents a byzantine scheme, recalling the scenes of the Giudgment of the damaged small table of Victoria and Albert Museum of London and the ones of the great picture of Vatican picture-gallery, in 1040-1080, and the fresco of S. Angelo in Formis, and other East interpretations like the one of Vorónet in Bucovina of the XIIth cent. West iconographic motives, due to the currents of the Benedectine painting and to subjects of the Gallican liturgy of the dead are included here, in Torcello, on these east schemes. Later the mosaicists ceased every activity in Torcello. Perhaps an economic crisis or the necessity of propping

37 - Detail of the « Doomsday » - Christ's descent to the Limbo

+HANAC ⁙

38 - Detail of the « Doomsday » - The Victorious Messiah

39/40 Detail of the « Doomsday » - The two Archangels' solemn figures - Above, Archangel Gabriele, on the right Archangel Michele - They hold the labarum with the invocation « ATIOC » (The Holy) in their right hands, and the world in their hands

up the supporting-walls of the central nave of the cathedral suggested to stop the works. On the other side the full decorative development of S. Mark's cathedral in Venice, needed the mosaic workmen. They, probably, went to S. Mark's to continue their « stil nuovo » (new style) inside it.

Near the entrance door there is the stoup (IXth cent.), whose basin is supported by a niello column from where four monstrous animals and four masks hang: the support capital is formed by four human figures, with long tunics, acting as caryatids (XIth-XIIth cent.).

Now the sacristy is used also as Museum of the Cathedral. Among its most important things there are, on the walls, some original pieces of the mosaic of the final judgement, before they were replaced by the present ones in the restoration at the end of the XIXth cent., and the oil series of the twelve Apostles, on canvas, in the inside side of the partition wall, a mediocre work of an anonym of the XVIIth cent. The processional silver cross of the XIIIth cent., and the series of statues, among which the Annunciation (XIIIth cent.) and the Madonna with the Child with a tiara on her head, a rare example of the XIVth cent., of the Virgin considered as Pontifex, have a particular interest. Besides there are the Crucifix of the XVIth cent. and the image of S. Fosca in the peace of death (XVth cent.).

Outside, go on, along the south side of the Cathedral, rising on a big stone base grazing the present parsonage, that is a change of the XVIIth cent. of the ancient episcopate and look at the ten windows of the central nave, open only on this side for light and climate purposes. The harmonious sequence of the apses and back facade opens on the east side.

The ample central apse has got a small apse below, and in the middle a window protected by the defensive lath from waters; from the base four pillars rise; each of the two side apses shows the elegant decoration with four pillars, enlivening the whole surface with a subtle play of motion and colour, repeating the motive of the facade and concluding with a stone small bracket with crosslet.

In the right small aisle the windows are six; the first and the last are without any shutters while the others have a square opening and peculiar shutters, i.e. of Istria stone movable on two big pivots, used, perhaps, in default of panes and for safety. Then you can see the large niche with remains of a fresco of the XIVth cent. All the perimetric wall is divided by big pillars to lighten and decorate the mass of building of barbaric taste. As to the date they saw, in the central apse, probable remains of the VIIth cent., heightened in 1008, while they thought the two side ones of the IXth cent. changed in Orseolo's time, i.e. in 1008 and carried out in different periods, considering the different level of the upper decoration.

In the upper part of the central nave there is a system of blind gallery, formed by five large niches, where the second are double-arched and the central one is very deep. You can see the motive of the facade pillars but here it is resolved in rather plastic values and of a marked roman taste, wheretofore the late decorative whole ranges itself mostly with S. Donato's in Murano. The fourth apse is not in keeping with the rest in fact it was added later, perhaps in full roman period, divided into six pillars.

On its side there is the large quadrangular bell-tower (55 ms. high) of the XIIth cent. near the most ancient lagoon bell-towers in style with the conduit divided into two compartments by a deep « lesenatura » with double small arches and six centring loop-holes in every side but closed on the north one. The cell is formed of three small columns of the same style of the outside ones of S. Fosca with three heraldic bearings on the west side of the XVIth cent. i.e., Torcello; the episcopal heraldic bearings of the Bishop Girolamo de Porcia (1516) and another one with some Keys. Two plait crosses, coeval of the bell-tower are inserted in the upper part of the cell. Above the entrance door there is a roman memorial tablet, inserted in 1008. The inside is characterized by large superposed arches, and by flights of steps you can reach the cell of bells, from where you enjoy the great loneliness of lagoons and sandy grounds, full of sun, green and waters, surrounded by roads and groves. Medieval towers generally testify the power of the town. Here, in Torcello, it gives the same impression of Pomposa and Aquileia, of which it is coeval. Then there is the small chapel consecrated to S. Mark, as, according to the text of the traslatio of the Xth cent., the remains of the Saint stayed here. Its plan repeats a very ancient scheme, i.e. the two side aisles were semicircular and the central one rectangular: the perimetric wall is rectilinear. They are the typical, architectonic forms of the Adriatic zone i.e. the hall-church lacking in apses, going back to the Vth or VIth cent. in Grado and somewhere else and to 1000 and later in Venice and here.

Nay the hint to the small church of the text of S. Mark's traslatio, of the XIth cent., leads us to suppose the building is of this period. Turn to the north and observe the decoration of the sacristy wall and treasure (erected in the XVIth cent.) in the terminal side westward, was interpreted in romanesque « revival » with pillar and upper small arches. So you come back to the grassy central square and can admire S. Fosca.

42 - The strange lockings of the Istrian-stone pane windows

◀
41 - The holy-water basin of the XIth cent. near the central door of the Cathedral

S. Fosca's

The building, miracolously saved by the destruction decided in 1811 by the French Government, rises on the right of the Cathedral, which it joins by a portico built in the XVIth cent. They thought the baptistery consecrated to S. Giovanni Battista had been built here in 639 and that it was used for the holy rites of the Christian communities running away from Altino. But there are no proofs of this ancient building. Now, the present one is consecrated to S. Fosca, from Ravenna, moved here, before 1011 from the oasis of Sabrata, in Libia, as tradition reports.

We don't know the shape of the more ancient building, acting as martyrium to keep the martyr's remains according to a common scheme in the architectonic complexes of late ancient times and upper Middle Ages.

Bettini states the present building, considering the architectonic profile, is of the XIIth cent.

It presents a very characteristic plan, according to the scheme of the crosswise churches with angle trumptes, like the ones of the byzantine area from Morea to Macedonia: the presbytery and three aisles with apses (the two side ones are the half of the central one) open on the central square room. The two side ones continue in a corridor near the central room; it repeats itself outside acting as polygonal narthex.

From the central flight of stairs you reach the brick, fishbone paved portico, formed of thirteen columns; five of them are polygonal, differently distributed; four are on the entrance side

In former times the columns were joined at their bases by marble plutei, as it appears on the first left side. The cross vault portico insists on the capitals, of different hand and style, which rest on the high structure and recalls similar methods in the Venetian-byzantine arcades of the following centuries in some Venetian palaces (Cà Loredan).

A woody angel of the XVIth cent, rests on the architrave of the central door; on the sides of the door there are two rests of Torcello buildings, one with a small palm, the other with vine-tendrils, works of byzantine taste of the XIIth cent. On the north side there is the high relief with S. Fosca venerated by her brethren, of 1407. Above the portico you can notice the architectonic play harmony of the domes and buttresses. The dome dominates solemn and calm with the hexagonal sail roof and the three centring windows to illuminate the inside and to colour the outside, interrupting the monotony of the whole. The dome rests on four side half-domes insisting on four right angle sectors, driven in four shed facades, with an evident function of push to the mass of building.

All the facades show a white cross with *manus Dei* (God's hand) in the middle of it, to increase the bright, sacred sense of the outside. It lacks the facade for the push on the east side, but in it this function is performed by the complex of the presbytery and the apses, that extends more, considering the plan, because of static purposes. All this system was conceived to build on it a large vault dome, which was never carried out, lest it might fall, as it happened in the similar buildings of greek area, so they decided to build a timber vault with a tile dome. When you enter the stone building, you feel conquered by the gravity and simplicity of the whole, which is the result of a complex play of architectonic elements.

43 - *S. Fosca's Church - A central plan building of the XI-XIIth cent.; surrounded, outside, on five sides, by a porch. It is a unique jewel in Italy like S. Sofia in Costantinopoli.*

▶

44 - *In the following page there are the « square » of Torcello and the surviving monuments of the island: the Cathedral, S. Fosca's and the ancient Archives*

From the central square room you pass into the round dome, resting on four, large pillars, in the four corners where arcades cross one another. The presbytery (with a large apse) very deep and delimited by two small aisles, continuing in the rest of the building by the marble columns of Cicladi, opens on the east of the central room; on the whole there are twelwe columns with fine corinthian capitals. If they had not used chains as tie-rods, the sense of space would appear more harmonious to show « that great, cultural refinement » Bettini speaks of, in a better way. The only present altar, turned to people, was built in 1970 with marbles of the isle of Marmara, in Ellesponto, in place of the one of the XVIIth cent. put in the Cathedral sacristy in 1915.

On the left side a painting in bad condition represents S. Fosca's martyrdom, a work of the mannerist Giulio del Moro (died in 1610), once on the altar of the XVIIth cent. In the apse you can see the beautiful Virgin with Child perhaps a work of the Ligurian school of the XVIth cent., near the Gagini. On the right there is the tabernacle, to keep the Holy Communion, a work of Remigio Barbaro, still alive.

Along the apse and the upper part of the presbytery, it runs a marble decoration of Cicladi, coeval of the church building.

In the left wall, on high, there is a very ruined painting with the « Assunta » in the middle, S. Fosca ans S. Maura on the right, S. Liberale and S. Eliodoro on the left, a work of a mannerist of the late XVIth cent. On the right wall there is a small votive icon of madonero (XVth cent.) with the Virgin and Child and S. Giacomo di Compostella. On the floor there are three tomb-stones; the one of the podesta of Torcello's daughter (died in 1705); Giovanni Tagliapietra, dean of Torcello's (died in 1753); Gerolamo Cambrotto, local dean's (died in 1696). In the sacristy, added long afterwards the construction of the church and presenting a fine small Sail bell tower, of lagoon style on the south side, that you can reach through a side small door, there are on the wall three remains of transept partition walls, decorated with birds, pecking among the vine-shoots, a fine decorative work, perhaps of the cathedral of the IXth cent. and a fine specimen of woody Crucifix of the XIVth cent. Outside the building, on the north side there is a large niche with three important frescoes of the XIVth cent., with the Crucifixion, three saints, and S. Cristoforo, acting as defence as, those who, going out of the cathedral could observe him, got protection all day long, according to the principles of medieval piety; a sarcopragus with an inscription in honour of Iacomele da Gaggio, cirùco (surgeon) died on March 20th 1426. Outside you can admire the three back apses, forming one of the best examples of the exarch style. The central one is pentagonal, divided into two orders; the inferior is formed by a false portico, got by five arcades, resting on double polygonal columns of the byzantine capital; in the upper one the arches resolve in pillars, on the countrary the central one, acting as a window, is very deep and with a double « risega » (step). The upper part of the central apse has a saw and wolf tooth decoration, of barbaric taste, surrounded by two indented fascias. The raceme central arch has in the middle, within a shield, the blessing *manus Dei* raised on high, a motive repeated in the plait crosses inserted in the facade buttresses. On the contrary on the two minor small apses there is no decoration, with the exception of the ample double-moulded pillar, containing the small, central window.

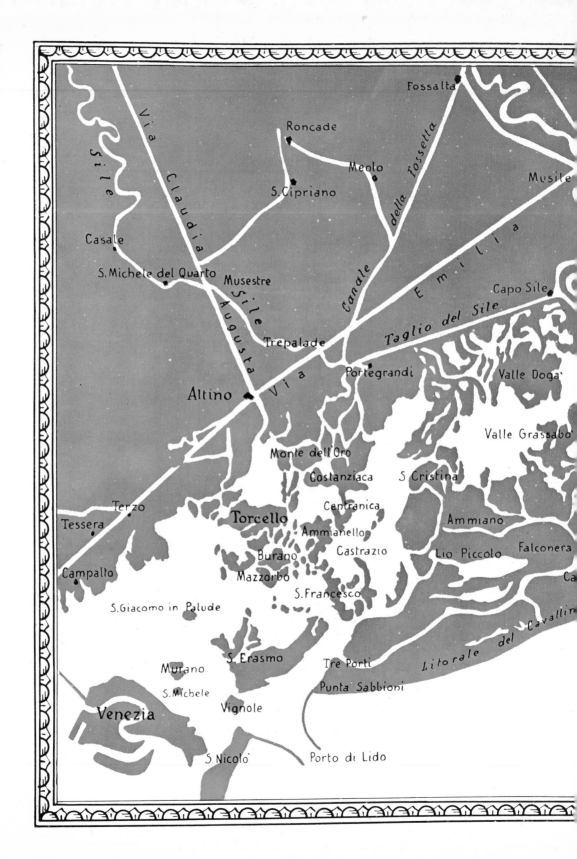

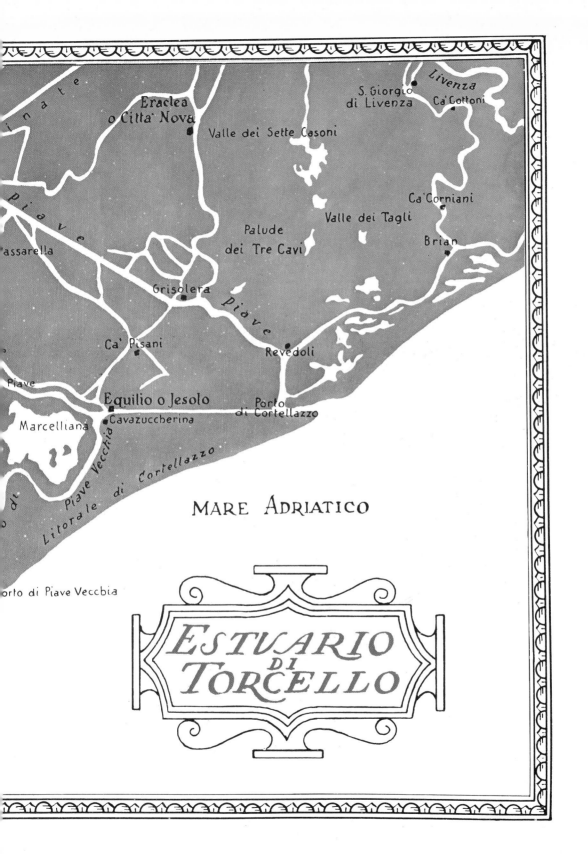

ESTUARIO DI TORCELLO

The list of the Deans of Torcello

The diocese of Torcello was suppressed in 1818 and the series of deans, presented here conformably to the data of the Archives of the Patriarch's court of Venice, began

Andrea Minio renounces on February 17th 1822
Pietro Giannelli, June 4th 1822 - died on October 2nd 1828
Luigi Stiore, December 5th 1828 - December 14th 1833
Pietro Simoncin, April 13th 1834 - died on February 18th 1837
Pier Antonio Paulini, April 14th 1837 - December 1st 1845
Francesco Pavan, May 1st 1846 - November 1st 1860
Francesco Bertola, October 23rd 1862 - died on September 30th 1869
Pietro Fratin, April 7th 1865 - December 17th 1868
Giuseppe Meneguzzi, March 22nd 1869 - January 2nd 1873
Tomaso Bertato, April 8th 1873 - February 17th 1876
Francesco Pagamuzzi, April 24th 1876 - August 22nd 1879
Gianfrancesco Zulian, November 18th 1881 - February 9th 1895
Allano Seno, April 8th 1895 - December 22nd 1904
Ettore Manzoni, May 20th 1910 - April 28th 1919
Spiridione Lazzari, June 1st 1920 - 1925
Francesco Tagliapietra, 1925 - 1951
Giovanni Cristofoli, 1952 - 1962
Mario Ferrarese, 1963 ad multos annos

Essential Bibliography

As to the bibliography preceding 1939 you can consult the very good book *of* G. LORENZETTI, *Torcello. La sua storia, i suoi monumenti*, Venezia 1939.
As to problems on architecture and mosaic decoration there is the good book: *Torcello*, Venezia 1940, by M. BRUNETTI, S. BETTINI, F. FORLATI, G. FIOCCO.
If you want to get a whole vision of all the problems of the Cathedral and S. Fosca's there is the essay of M. BRUNETTI, Torcello, in « Storia di Venezia », II, *Dalle origini del Ducato alla IV crociata*, Venezia 1958, pp. 597-621. As to the Roman installation problems you can see: L. LECIEJEWICZ, E. TABACZYNSKA, S. TABACZYNSKI, *Ricerche archeologiche nell'area della Cattedrale di Torcello nel 1965*, « Bollettino dell'Istituto di Storia della Società e dello Stato Veneziano », III (1961), pp. 37-47; *Ricerche archeologiche a Torcello nel 1962. Relazione provvisoria*, « Bollettino », cit. V-VI (1963-64) pp. 3-14. On the christian origins: A. PERTUSI, *L'iscrizione torcellana dei tempi di Eraclio*, « Bollettino », cit. IV, (1962) pp. 9-38. As to a too radical interpretation of the apse and diaconicon mosaics; A.M. DAMIGELLA, *Problemi della Cattedrale di Torcello*, I, *I Mosaici dell'abside destra*, « Commentari », XVII (1966), pp. 3-15; II, The Mosaics of the « maggior » apse, « Commentari », XVIII (1967), pp. 273-289; for a general vision: V. LAZAREV, *Storia della pittura bizantina*, Torino 1967, pp. 242, 271. For the mosaic iconologic calls you can consult: G. TOSCANO, *Il pensiero cristiano nell'arte*, Bergamo 1960, I, pp. 323, 360, 370, 394-398, II, 151.

Index of the Illustrations

Lire 1500